Introduction

contents

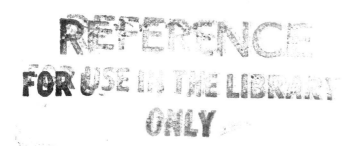

© Maureen Lewis
& David Wray
EXEL – Exeter Extending
Literacy project.

ISBN 0-704-91064-0

Reading and Language
Information Centre
The University of Reading
Bulmershe Court
Earley
Reading RG6 1HY

This publication was first
produced as part of the
EXEL (The Exeter Extending
Literacy) project funded by
the Nuffield Foundation.

We would like to thank the
many teachers and children
throughout the country who
have trialled writing frames
in their classrooms. Their
insights, expertise, sugges-
tions and critical support
have been invaluable.

We would particularly
like to thank the following
Devon teachers who were
all members of our Genre
Group and gave freely of
their time, their ideas and
their classroom experience:

Carolyn Ballard
*Bishopsteignton
Primary School*

Margaret Birch
Manor Primary School

Andrea Bradshaw
*Bere Alston County
Primary School*

Caroline Cox
Stoke Hill First

Rosie Culverhouse
Tavistock Community College

David Edwards
*Cheriton Bishop
Primary School*

Jan Marshall
*Horrabridge County
Primary School*

Patricia Rospigliosi
*Learning support teacher
West Devon*

Chris Stratton
Alphington Combined School

National Curriculum English
documents (DES 1990; DfEE 1995)
have made it clear that children
should undertake a wide range of
different types of writing and that
they should be 'helped to plan and
produce these types of writing' –
descriptions, explanations, opinions,
etc – 'by being given purposeful
opportunities to write their own'.
In spite of the many changes to the
English orders over the last few years,
the emphasis on non-fiction writing
remains a recurrent theme ①.

The EXEL (Exeter Extending
Literacy) project attempted to
address this issue by developing
'writing frames' which would act as
a kind of scaffolding for children's
non-fiction writing. The frames have
been trialled with children throughout the country in primary and lower
secondary years and across the full
range of abilities, including children
with special needs.

① 'Pupils should be able to … produce a
range of types of non-chronological writing.'
English in the national curriculum
(DES 1990; AT3, level 3d)

'Pupils should … be taught to write in a range
of forms, incorporating some of the different
characteristics of those forms.'
Key stages 1 and 2 of the national curriculum
(DfEE 1995: 9)

This publication sets out to:

- explain the history and purposes
  of writing frames

- outline the characteristics of
  six different non-fiction genres –
  recount, report, explanation,
  procedure, persuasion and
  discussion

- give examples of how writing
  frames scaffold children's writing
  in each of these genres

- offer blank templates (see pages
  16–39) which can be used in a range
  of situations.

Writing frames

Non-fiction writing is generally felt to be more problematic for children than more familiar narrative texts because of linguistic features such as the use of specialist vocabulary, structures and connectives. Consequently, they need more support to produce their own non-fiction writing.

Genre analysis undertaken by Australian researchers offers an exciting way forward. Six main genres will be considered in this publication – recount, report, procedure, explanation, persuasion and discussion. Analysis of the typical structure of these different genres has helped to shape the writing frames developed as part of the EXEL project ②.

Writing frames are templates consisting of starters, connectives and sentence modifiers which offer children a structure for communicating what they want to say. They help by

- giving experience of a range of generic structures
- providing the cohesive links which allow children to maintain the sense of what they are writing
- offering a varied vocabulary of connectives and sentence beginnings which allow children to go beyond the familiar *and then…*

② For a more detailed explanation of genre analysis, see Lewis, M. & Wray, D. (1995) *Developing children's non-fiction writing.* Leamington Spa: Scholastic

③ Vygotsky, L. (1978) *Mind in society: the development of higher psychological processes.* Cambridge Mass: Harvard University Press

- encouraging a personal interpretation of information gathered through the careful use of personal pronouns
- asking children to select and think about what they have learnt by re-ordering information and demonstrating their understanding, rather than just copying out text
- ensuring some success at writing, a vital ingredient in improving self-esteem and motivation
- providing an alternative to a blank sheet of paper – a particularly daunting experience, especially for children who find sustained writing difficult
- giving children an overview of the writing task.

A model for teaching

The model of teaching upon which we have based the work of the EXEL Project can be summarised in FIGURE 1 below.

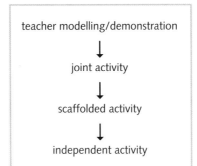

teacher modelling/demonstration
↓
joint activity
↓
scaffolded activity
↓
independent activity

FIGURE 1
The EXEL teaching model

This model arises from Vygotsky's (1978) ideas on how children learn in collaboration with experts – parents or teachers. At first they are spectators and most of the cognitive work is done by the expert. As they grow in experience and capability, the expert passes over greater and greater responsibility but still acts as a guide, assisting the child at problematic points. Eventually, the child assumes full responsibility for the task with the expert still present in the role of a supportive audience ③.

This model makes good theoretical sense but can be a little difficult to apply in a busy, over-populated classroom where children are often expected to move into independent writing before they are really ready. A 'scaffolded phase' is clearly needed to span joint and independent activity, where children are offered strategies to aid writing which they can use without an adult necessarily being alongside them. Writing frames are one such strategy. They act both as a way of increasing a child's experience of a particular type of non-fiction writing and as a substitute for teacher intervention.

How to use the frames

Use of the frame should always begin with discussion and teacher modelling before moving on to joint construction (teacher plus child/children) and then to independent writing supported by the frame. This pattern of teaching is vital, for it not only

models the generic form and teaches the words that signal connections and transitions, but also provides opportunities for developing children's thinking and oral language. Some children, and especially those with learning difficulties, may need many oral sessions and sessions where the teacher acts as a scribe before they attempt their own writing.

'Big' versions of the frames can be used in the teacher modelling and joint construction phases. It is important that both child and teacher understand that the frame should be used as a support for drafting – words may be crossed out or changed, extra sentences may be added and surplus starters crossed out. The frame should not be treated as a strait-jacket.

When to use the frames

Writing in a range of genres is most effective if it is located in meaningful experiences. For this reason, the frames should always be used as part of class topic work rather than in isolated study skills lessons. Much primary school teaching is still largely based on this model of curriculum planning and we would argue very strongly for its potential effectiveness. The frame itself never offers a purpose for writing.

When children do have a reason for writing, there are several situations where you may decide it is appropriate to offer a frame:

- when they first attempt independent writing in an unfamiliar genre

- when they appear stuck in a particular mode of writing, eg constantly using 'and then' … 'and then'
- when they wander between genres in a way that demonstrates a lack of understanding, eg procedural texts such as recipes may start in a second person or instructional mode (*First you beat the egg*) but then shift into a recount (*Next I stirred in the flour*). Mixing genres can, of course, be a deliberate and creative decision, and we must take care to differentiate between those occasions when children purposely move between genres and those where different genres are confused
- when they have written something in one genre which would be more appropriate in another genre, eg reporting an experiment as a personal recount.

In all of these situations it is important to stress that writing frames are just one of a range of strategies and writing experiences which teachers would offer children.

Using the frames with a range of writers

The frames are helpful for children of all ages and abilities from ks1 to ks3. However, they are particularly useful with children of average writing ability and with those who find writing difficult.

Children already confident and fluent in a particular genre clearly need no further scaffolding in that genre. However, writing frames can be used to extend their experience to other genres. While teachers sometimes note an initial dip in the quality of the writing, the new genre and its language features are often added to the repertoires of confident writers after only one or two uses of a frame.

Moving from frame to independent writing

As children become familiar with a frame, they should be encouraged to make additions or deletions. For example, Robert (aged 9) had more to say than the frame allowed and so he continued to add to it (see FIGURE 2). It is noticeable that he continues to use appropriate connectives and maintains the textual cohesion. The initial scaffolding has begun to give way to independent usage. This indicates he is probably ready to move to the independent phase. The length of time that children feel the need to use a frame will, of course, vary from individual to individual.

Later, as children begin to show evidence of independent usage, they can consult copies of the frames placed in a box of help cards in the writing area. This form of support also encourages them to start making independent decisions about their own learning.

Remember

- use of the frame should always take the following sequence
  - discussion and teacher modelling
  - joint construction (teacher plus child/group)
  - independent writing supported by the frame
- not all the children in a class will need to use a writing frame
- writing frames should only be used when children have a purpose for writing
- children should be encouraged to cross out, amend and add to the frame as suits them
- frames are only a small part of the varied and rich writing experiences we offer children
- generic structures are not rigid, unchangeable forms
- the frames in this book are starting points which teachers can develop for their own unique classroom contexts and purposes.

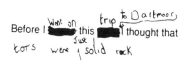

FIGURE 2
Writing produced by Robert, a Year 4 child: initial draft with independently added connectives underlined.

Recount genre frames

**Recounts inform or entertain their audience –
or even both! – by retelling events.**

Recounts usually consist of
- **orientation**: a 'scene setting' opening, eg *I went on a visit to the museum, Our class planted some seeds*
- **events**: a recount of the events as they occurred, eg *I sat with Sarah on the bus, We put soil in four pots*
- **reorientation**: a closing statement, eg *When we got back from the trip we wrote about it, The seeds with soil, light and water grew best.*

Recounts are often written in the past tense, with events presented in chronological order. They focus on individual participants and use 'doing/action' clauses.

Recount frames are often the most successful way of introducing the frames: they clearly direct the children's attention to the topic and, through the use of the personalised sentence structure, make them active participants, using their own voices (see, for example, FIGURE 3). Writing from personal experience is a very important part of children's writing development.

Most children already write many recounts and are very familiar with this genre. The frames given here may therefore be most useful in offering alternative starters and connectives and encouraging children to write in different ways. Seven alternative recount frames are offered:
- prior knowledge and reaction
- prior knowledge and reaction (visit)
- prior knowledge and revision
- prior knowledge and revision (visit)
- sequential
- enumeration
- enumeration (visit).

These photocopiable frames are on pages 17–23.

FIGURE 3
An example of recount writing produced by a Year 4 child.

Our trip to Exeter Museum.

On Tuesday the 1st February we went on a school trip to a Roman museum in Exeter. — **orientation**

First of all we split in to two groups. Then my group went upstairs. We looked at Roman tiles, bits of pottery, jawbones, a deer antler, a coin, sheep bone and a bit of mosaic. We saw a tile which, before it was baked, a dog had walked over and it had paw prints on it. Then we went downstairs into the Roman kitchen which had been reconstructed from information from the ground. We did some observational drawings. Then we each had a turn at grinding the flour. The guide who took us around told us to look for a mysterious animal that the romans ate. I was the first person to find out what it was. It was a hedgehog. — **events**

Then we went to another museum. It was much better than the first because the man who took us round was funny and we were allowed to try on Roman armour. We handled the weapons as well. There was a sword, a dagger and a pilon. The armour was a breast plate, a shield, a helmet and a belt made with leather and chingles. The bits they hadn't got were the helmet, dagger and shield. Then we looked at part of a mosaic. Then we went home.

It was a good trip. I liked the armour. — **reorientation**

Prior knowledge and reaction frame

This frame encourages children to base their accounts on what they have learnt rather than what they did and offers them an alternative structure to a chronological recount. Pupils give their opinion of the information they wish to recount eg *the most interesting thing I learnt* (see FIGURE 4).

Prior knowledge and revision frame

The prior knowledge plus revision frame helps children to reflect on anything they have discovered which conflicts with or supplements what they already knew. Getting children to acknowledge and change their misconceptions is difficult. They will often ignore information that contradicts what they already know. This frame can be used to acknowledge such conflicts or to add further detail to existing knowledge (see FIGURE 5).

FIGURE 4
Writing with a prior knowledge and reaction frame by a Year 4 child with specific learning difficulties, after watching a video and group discussion.

FIGURE 5
Writing produced by a Year 5 child after collecting information from books.

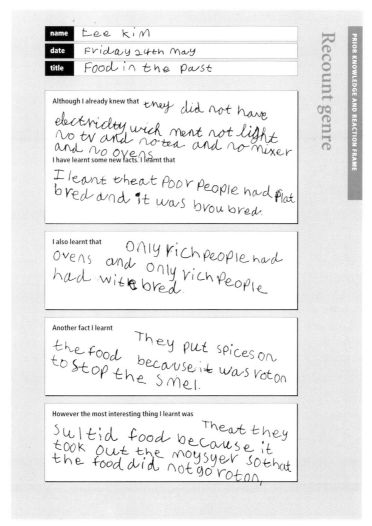

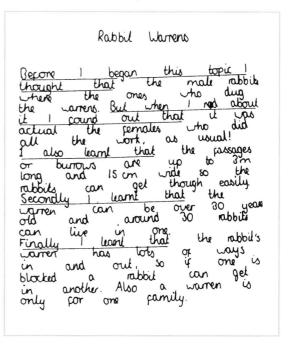

Prior knowledge and reaction/revision visit frames

As we can see in FIGURE 6, these frames can transform a 'bed to bed retelling' (*I got up and had my breakfast … then we ate our sandwiches … then we went back to school…*) into a personalised, detailed account of what has been learnt.

Sequential frames

Recounts are usually chronological in order, ie they are told in the time sequence in which they took place. This often means that children adopt an 'and then, and then, and then' mode of writing. The sequential frame offers more interesting alternatives. It also offers a logical structure to help those children who find it hard to hold a sequence. In the example of children's work shown in FIGURE 7 the given frame is underlined.

FIGURE 6
Writing produced using a prior knowledge and reaction (visit) frame by a Year 5 child after a visit to a museum.

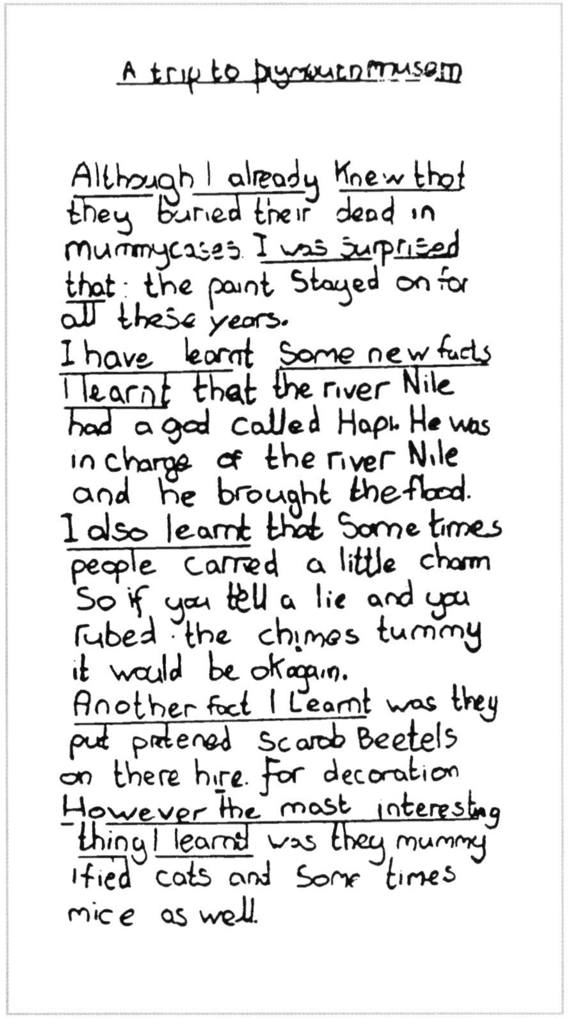

A trip to plymouth musem

Although I already knew that they buried their dead in mummycases. I was surprised that the paint stayed on for all these years.
I have learnt some new facts I learnt that the river Nile had a god called Hapi. He was in charge of the river Nile and he brought the flood.
I also learnt that sometimes people carried a little charm so if you tell a lie and you rubed the chimes tummy it would be ok again.
Another fact I learnt was they put pretened scarob Beetels on there hire. For decoration However the most interesting thing I learnt was they mummyified cats and sometimes mice as well.

FIGURE 7
An alternative structure to a chronological recount completed by a Year 2 child after previous shared writing experiences using sequential frames.

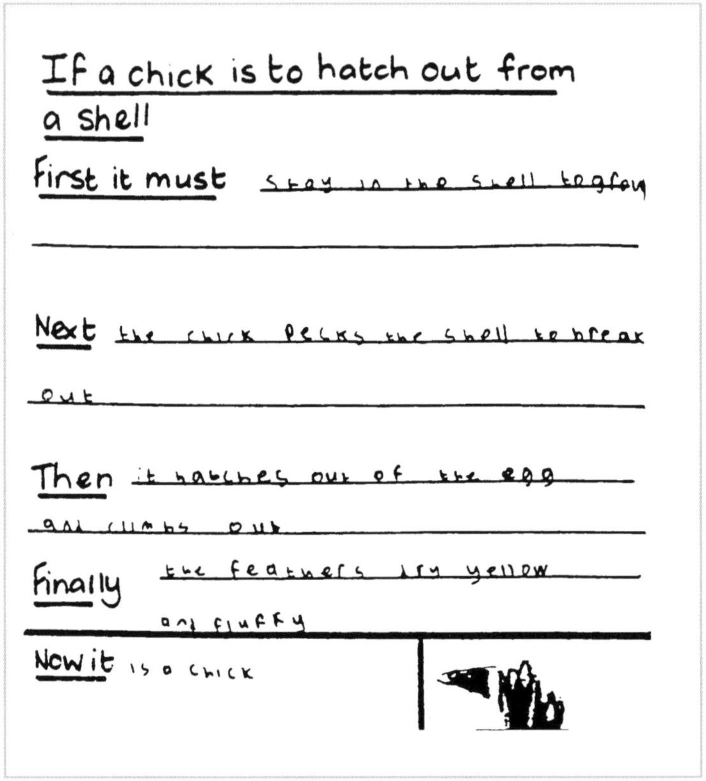

If a chick is to hatch out from a shell
First it must stay in the shell to grow

Next the chick pecks the shell to break out

Then it hatches out of the egg and climbs out

Finally the feathers dry yellow and fluffy

Now it is a chick

Enumeration frame

Listing is an early genre familiar for most children. The enumeration frame uses this familiar form to enhance recount writing. Most children find this an easily accessible format. Many teachers also encourage the use of this frame to summarise the end of a term's work, as we see in Hannah's recount in FIGURE 8.

FIGURE 8
Writing produced by a Year 5 child using an enumeration frame to summarise and reflect on her work on the Romans.

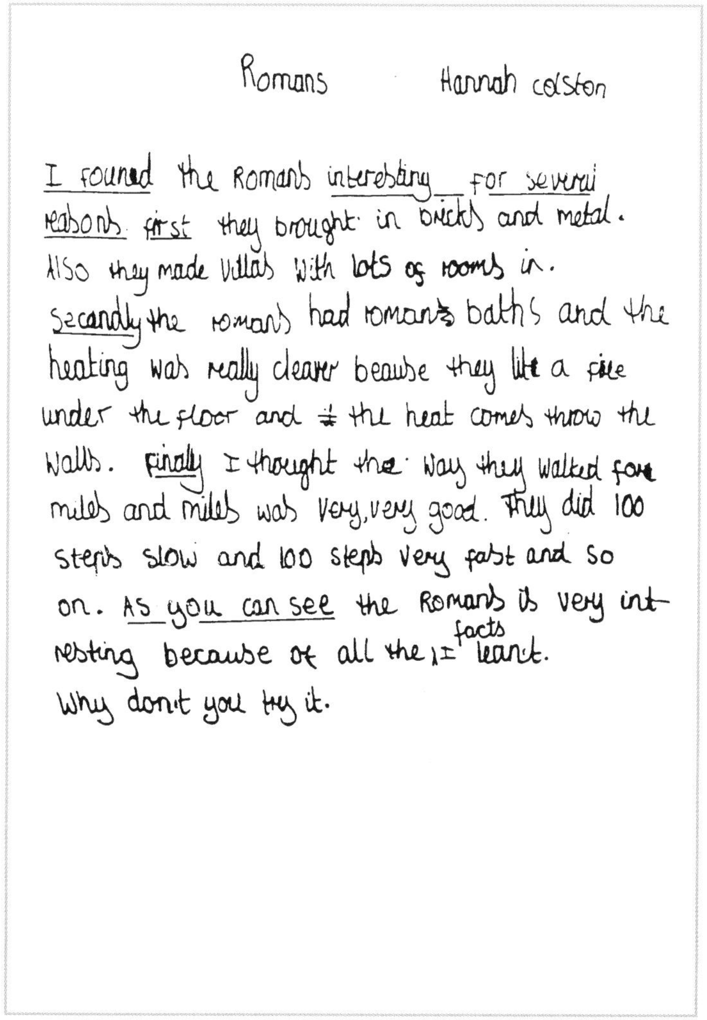

Romans   Hannah colston

I founed the Romans interesting for several reasons. first they brought in bricks and metal. Also they made villas with lots of rooms in. Secondly the romans had romans baths and the heating was really clearer because they lite a fire under the floor and the heat comes throw the walls. finally I thought the way they walked for miles and miles was very, very good. they did 100 steps slow and 100 steps very fast and so on. As you can see the Romans is very interesting because of all the facts I learnt. Why don't you try it.

Report genre frames

Reports describe a range of natural, cultural or social phenomena.

Reports usually consist of

■ an opening, general classification, eg *Exeter is a city in Devon, Humans are mammals*

■ a more technical classification (optional), eg *A city holds a Royal Charter, The scientific name is 'Homo sapiens'*

■ a description of the phenomenon in question, eg *qualities*, *parts and their function*, *habits*, *behaviour or uses*. They are usually written in the present tense, are non-chronological, focus on groups of things (generic participants) and use 'being' and 'having' clauses, as we see in Simon's report in FIGURE 9.

FIGURE 9
An example of report writing produced by Simon, a Year 6 child.

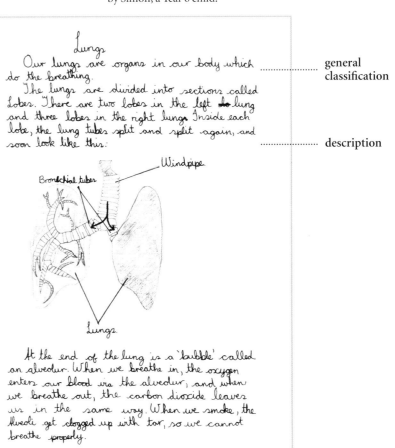

general classification

description

Comparison and contrast frames

These are more complex versions of reports. An opening statement introduces the general classification. This is followed by a description of the similarities and differences, eg *Although Exeter and London are both cities, they are different in many ways….*

Comparing and contrasting phenomena is a sophisticated skill for which most children require support. Before attempting the frame children will need to use some kind of graphic organiser like the grid provided (see FIGURE 10). This enables them to organise a mass of information before they begin writing. Later, they proceed to use this information in continuous writing. FIGURE 11, for instance, is an example of independent writing after experience of using a comparison frame.

FIGURE 10

A comparison grid completed by a Year 4 child before using a writing frame.

Report genre

COMPARISON GRID

name	Samantha Green
date	Friday 14th June
title	Food in Ancient Greece and Today

What to do:
- Write the names of the objects being compared/contrasted in boxes A and B below – for example A: *My house*, B: *Victorian house.*
- List the characteristics being studied in the boxes in the left hand column – for example *heating, lighting, cooking facilities, building materials.*
- Use the grid to record information before writing a report.

characteristics	A What I ate Yesterday	B What the Greeks ate
Breakfast	Nothing	Bread and fruit or a lump of bread soaked in wine
Lunch	Pasta and cheese and potatoes.	Bread with a peice of cheese or some olives and figs.
Evening meal	Fish and chips bread and butter and tomato sauce	vegetables fish meat bread.
snacks	Apple crumble	Pomegranetes
Drinks	Tango and water	water milk and wine.

Grid for use before writing a comparison and contrast frames

FIGURE 11

Independent writing by a Year 5 child after previous experience of using a comparison frame. The child first filled in a grid. Note how the structure and language of the frame has been assimilated into her independent writing.

A comparison of a Middle Class Victorian home with a modern home

Victorian houses differ from modern houses in the way that the victorians had doorbells pulled with a rope however we have electric bells. Whilst the victorians had fancy doors most of us nowadays don't bother. Victorians liked flowers, because of this they used to decorate their houses with flower painting tiles, this does not differ much from the modern fashion of decorating kitchens and bathrooms with Floral tiles. The Victorians also used floral tiles to make their gardens paths prettier whilst modern houses don't do this. Victorian houses had big fire places and modern houses still do. Their walls had dado rails which stopped the furniture from rubbing against the wallpaper. Churches have stained glass windows which differ from the windows used in houses.

Explanation genre frames

This genre is used to explain natural and social phenomena.

FIGURE 12
An example of explanation writing
produced by Bill, a Year 5 child.

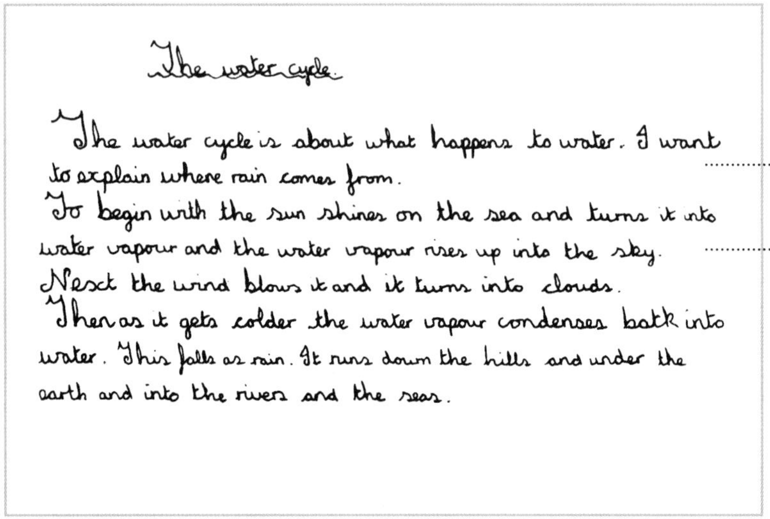

Explanations usually consist of
- a general statement to introduce the topic, eg *A butterfly goes through several stages in its life cycle*, *Computers use a binary number system*
- a series of logical steps explaining how or why something occurs. These steps continue until the final state is produced or the explanation is complete, eg *A goes through this process to become B, B then goes through this process to become C*, etc.

Explanations are often written in the simple present tense, using temporal (*then*, *next*, *after*, etc) and/or causal conjunctions (*because*, *therefore*, etc), and mainly 'action' clauses.

Some explanations contain elements of the sequential genre but are differentiated from simple sequential recounts by the use of causal statements. For an example of explanation, see FIGURE 12; and for examples of writing with explanation frames, see FIGURES 13 and 14.

In the photocopiable pages found at the end of this book, a choice of explanation frames is given. The first (page 27) is causal. The other two frames (pages 28–29) not only ask children to explain a phenomenon but also to ascribe value to differing explanations.

The water cycle

The water cycle is about what happens to water. I want to explain where rain comes from. .... opening statement

To begin with the sun shines on the sea and turns it into water vapour and the water vapour rises up into the sky. .... series of steps explaining the phenomena

Next the wind blows it and it turns into clouds.

Then as it gets colder the water vapour condenses back into water. This falls as rain. It runs down the hills and under the earth and into the rivers and the seas.

FIGURE 13
An example of writing with an explanation frame produced by a Year 4 child receiving individual language support.

FIGURE 14
An example of a writing with an explanation frame produced by a Year 4 child.

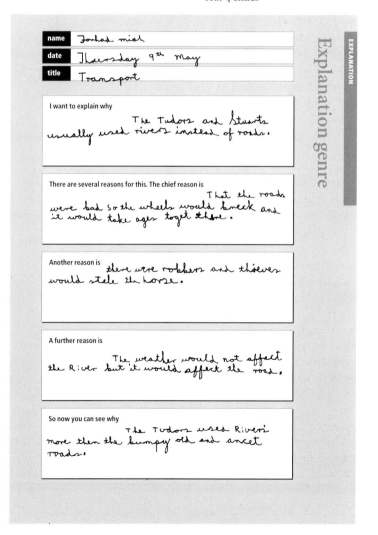

Procedure genre frames

Procedures or instructions are written to describe how something is done in a series of sequenced steps.

A procedural text usually consists of
- a statement of what is to be achieved, eg *How to make a cake*
- a list of materials/equipment needed to achieve the goal
- a series of sequenced steps to achieve the goal, eg *Cream the sugar and butter*
- in many cases, a diagram or illustration.

It is usually written in the simple present tense or using imperatives (*do this, do that*), is chronological, focuses on generalised human agents rather than individuals (*first you take* rather than *first I take*), and consists of mainly doing/action clauses. For an example of procedural writing, see FIGURE 15.

Procedural frames scaffold childrens' writing in the more formal register of instructions.

The first two procedural frames in the photocopiable section at the end of this book (pages 30–31) use the same generic structure but offer differing vocabulary and layout.

During the trialling of these frames many children commented on the need for diagrams to clarify their instructions. The third frame (page 32) allows for a more visual approach.

FIGURE 15
An example of procedural writing produced by Sarah, a Year 5 child.

> **Object of the game** — goal
>
> The object of the game is to get to the finesh with all the items.
>
> **Equipment** — materials and equipment
>
> For the game you will need:
> 1 Dice
> 2-4 counters
> the 15 item cards.
>
> **How to play** — steps to achieve the goal
>
> (1.) Each player choses a counter and the person who throws a 6 first starts.
> (2.) After you have thrown the dice move the number spaces it says on it.
> (3.) If you land on a shop pick one item card if not carry on. If you land on a space which says lose something place the item it says in the lost item space.
> (4.) If you have not got all the cards by the time you have got to the finesh keep going round until you have got them.
>
> This game is for 2-4 players.

Persuasion genre frames

Persuasive writing takes many forms from advertising copy to polemical pamphlets. Its purpose is to promote a particular point of view or argument – unlike a discussion paper which considers alternative points of view.

Persuasive writing usually consists of

- **the thesis**: an opening statement, often in the form of position/preview, eg *Fox hunting is a cruel and barbaric sport*

- **the arguments**: often in the form of point plus elaboration, eg *Foxes rarely attack domestic animals. Statistics show…*

- **reiteration**: a summary and restatement of the opening position, eg *We have seen that… Therefore, all the evidence points unmistakably to the conclusion that fox hunting is clearly cruel and unnecessary.*

It is usually written in the simple present tense, focusing mainly on generic human participants and using mostly logical rather than temporal conjunctions. For an example of persuasive writing see FIGURE 16; for an example of writing produced with a persuasive frame see FIGURE 17.

As with all the frames in this publication, discussion, teacher modelling and joint construction of texts are vital first stages. Many children will find some kind of preliminary organising of their main arguments such as the 'protest posters' frame (see page 33) a helpful first stage in recording their ideas and information.

FIGURE 16
An example of persuasive writing produced by James, a Year 5 child.

I think that building houses on the old school field is a bad thing.
I have several reasons for thinking this like the wildlife and the youth club.

     — thesis
     position

     — preview

My first reason is that it would be destroying wildlife on the field because of all the digging and when the people move in the noise, the light and other things.
A further reason is the youth club would not like it because they use the field for games and other things. And they might disturb the people in the houses.
Furthermore there are enough houses in the village. We do not need anymore. It would just be a waste of space (we need that space).

     — arguments
     point
     elaboration

     point
     elaboration

     point
     elaboration

Therefore although some people think it would t a good thing to because it would create more homes I think I have shown lots of reasons why it is not a very good thing to build more houses here especially on the old school field.

     — reiteration

FIGURE 17
Writing produced by a Year 7 child using a persuasion frame.

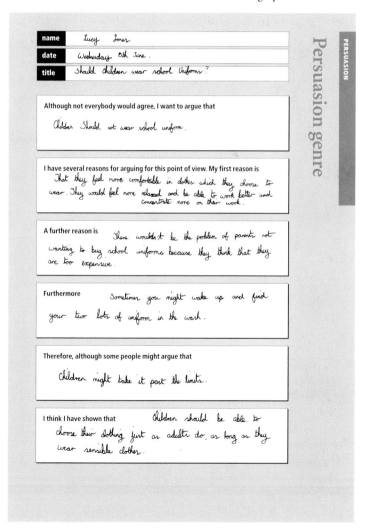

PERSUASION

Persuasion genre

name   Lucy   Jones

date   Wednesday 8th June.

title   Should children wear school Uniforms?

Although not everybody would agree, I want to argue that
Children should not wear school uniform.

I have several reasons for arguing for this point of view. My first reason is
that they feel more comfortable in clothes which they choose to wear. They would feel more relaxed and be able to work better and concentrate more on their work.

A further reason is There wouldn't be the problem of parents not wanting to buy school uniforms because they think that they are too expensive.

Furthermore Sometimes you might wake up and find your two lots of uniform in the wash.

Therefore, although some people might argue that
Children might take it past the limits.

I think I have shown that Children should be able to choose their clothing just as adults do, as long as they wear sensible clothes.

Discussion genre frames

Discussion papers are written to present arguments and information from differing viewpoints.

They usually consist of

- a statement of the issue plus pre-view of the main arguments, eg *Our school is trying to decide whether to have a uniform. Some people think it would improve the school whilst other groups that it is unnecessary*

- arguments for plus supporting evidence, eg *Most of the local schools already have a uniform and most of the children look very smart*

- arguments against plus supporting evidence, eg *Most of the pupils feel very strongly that not wearing uniform allows them to feel more individual and grown-up.* (The order of arguments for and against can, of course, be reversed)

- recommendation given as a summary and conclusion, eg *One group wants to unify the school whilst the other group claims freedom of choice…. I think….*

They are usually written in the simple present tense using generic human, or non-human participants, rather than personal pronouns (except in the conclusion) and use logical conjunctions (*therefore*, *because* etc). An example of discussion writing can be seen in FIGURE 18 opposite.

Children are increasingly expected to use this genre as they progress through the education system. Although the weighing of arguments backed by evidence before reaching a conclusion is used in secondary and higher education for the writing of academic essays, younger pupils often have very little experience of this genre.

Writing discussion papers can be a natural extension of the debate which is a feature of primary classrooms. A preliminary framework (see FIGURE 19) should be used after or alongside discussion. This can then be further refined into a completed piece of writing (see, for instance, FIGURE 20). Teachers can make their own giant versions on sugar paper or use an OHP for the initial teacher modelling/ joint construction phase. Gathering the information and organising it is a vital step before writing. Some teachers may feel that the preliminary frame-work itself is sufficient scaffold for further writing. Others may wish to use a discussion frame.

FIGURE 18
An example of discussion writing produced by Laura, a Year 6 child.

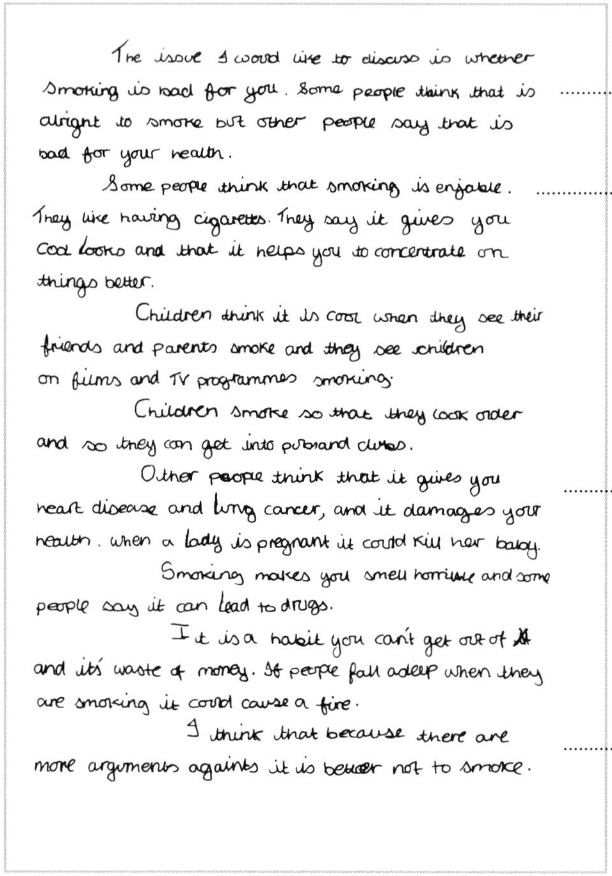

statement of issue preview

arguments for

arguments against

recommendation

FIGURE 19

A Year 4 child using the preliminary
frame for discussion writing.

FIGURE 20

Writing by a Year 6 child using
a discussion frame typed up on
the computer after producing a
handwritten first draft.

DISCUSSION

Discussion genre

name	Darren Horley
date	Friday 17th May
title	Zoo's

The issue we are discussing is whether
Whether Zoo's are good
or bad.

Make notes in the boxes below listing the arguments for and against.
■ Remember notes are just brief outlines. They don't have to be in sentences.

Arguments for

① Zoo's are good because the animals can not be hunted
② Zoo's are Good because they feed the animals well
③ Zoo's are good because they can be discovered. I think that Safari park's cleaner than Zoo's.

Arguments against

① Safari parks are Better than Zoos because the Safari parks have more space for the animals!
② Safari parks are better because they don't keep the animals in cages
③ Safari is better because in Zoos they can't be filmed.

My conclusion, based on the evidence, is
I think thats Zoos are better places for animals than Safari parks because animals cant be hunted.

Now use these notes to help you write a discussion paper on this issue

---

Our class have been debating whether football should only be allowed to be played in the school playground on Mondays, Wednesdays and Fridays because our playground is quite small in the winter when we can't use the field.

The people who don't like playing football say it is unfair that football takes up a lot of space in the playground. They say they cannot walk around because they get bumped into and hit with the ball. They also say it is scarey for little kids.

The footballers say that most people like playing so they should be allowed to. And if they cannot practice the school team will get worse and we won't win many games. Also they will not enjoy school if they cannot play with their friends.

I think that football should be allowed everyday because most people like it and it is good fun.

Photocopiable writing frames

Recount genre

name

date

title

Although I already knew that

I have learnt some new facts. I learnt that

I also learnt that

Another fact I learnt

However the most interesting thing I learnt was

Recount genre

name

date

title

Although I already knew that

I have learnt some new facts from our trip to ⋯⋯⋯⋯⋯⋯
I learnt that

I also learnt that

Another fact I learnt

However the most interesting thing I learnt was

Recount genre

name

date

title

Before I began this topic I thought that

But when I read about it I found out that

I also learnt that

Furthermore I learnt that

Finally I learnt that

Recount genre

name

date

title

Before I went on the visit to .... I thought that

But when I got there I found out that

I also learnt that

Another thing I learnt was that

Finally I learnt that

Recount genre

name

date

title

To begin with

Next

Then

After that

Finally

Now

Recount genre

name

date

title

I found .... interesting for several reasons.

I discovered that

I also learnt

It was interesting that

Finally

As you can see

Recount genre

name

date

title

I found our visit to .... interesting for several reasons. I discovered that

I also learnt

It was interesting that

Finally

As you can see

Grid for use before writing comparison and contrast reports

Report genre

name

date

title

What to do

■ Write the names of the objects being compared/contrasted in boxes A and B below – for example A: *My house*, B: *Victorian house*.

■ List the characteristics being studied in the boxes in the left hand column – for example *heating, lighting, cooking facilities, building materials*.

■ Use the grid to record information before writing a report.

characteristics	A	B

Report genre

name

date

title

Although .... and .... are .... different .... they are alike in some interesting ways.

For example they both

They are also similar in

The .... is the same as

The .... resembles

Finally they both

Report genre

name

date

title

Although .... and ....
are both .... they are different in many ways.
The .... has .... whilst
.... has ....

They are also different in that

Another way in which they differ is

Finally

Explanation genre

name

date

title

I want to explain how

To begin with / It starts by

And this makes / means / changes

After that

And as a result

Next

Then

The final result is that the

Explanation genre

name

date

title

There are differing explanations as to why / how / what / when

One explanation is that

The evidence for this is

An alternative explanation is

This explanation is based on

Of the alternative explanations I think the most likely is

Explanation genre

name

date

title

I want to explain why

There are several reasons for this. The chief reason is

Another reason is

A further reason is

So now you can see why

Procedure genre

name

date

title

How to

You will need

The stages

1 First you

2 Then you

3 Next

4

5

6

Procedure genre

name

date

title

Goal

Equipment and materials required

■ Use the box below to explain each stage – eg: 1. *First you…* 2. *Then…* 3. …. 4. ….

Action plan

Evaluation How far has the goal been achieved? Any further action to be taken?

Procedure genre

name

date

title

How to

You will need

■ Use the box below to put a drawing or diagram of what you are explaining

Diagram/drawing

■ Use the box below to explain each stage – eg 1.First you... 2. Then... 3. Next... Finally...

The stages

Persuasion genre

name

date

title

Write statements in the 'protest posters' to support your point of view

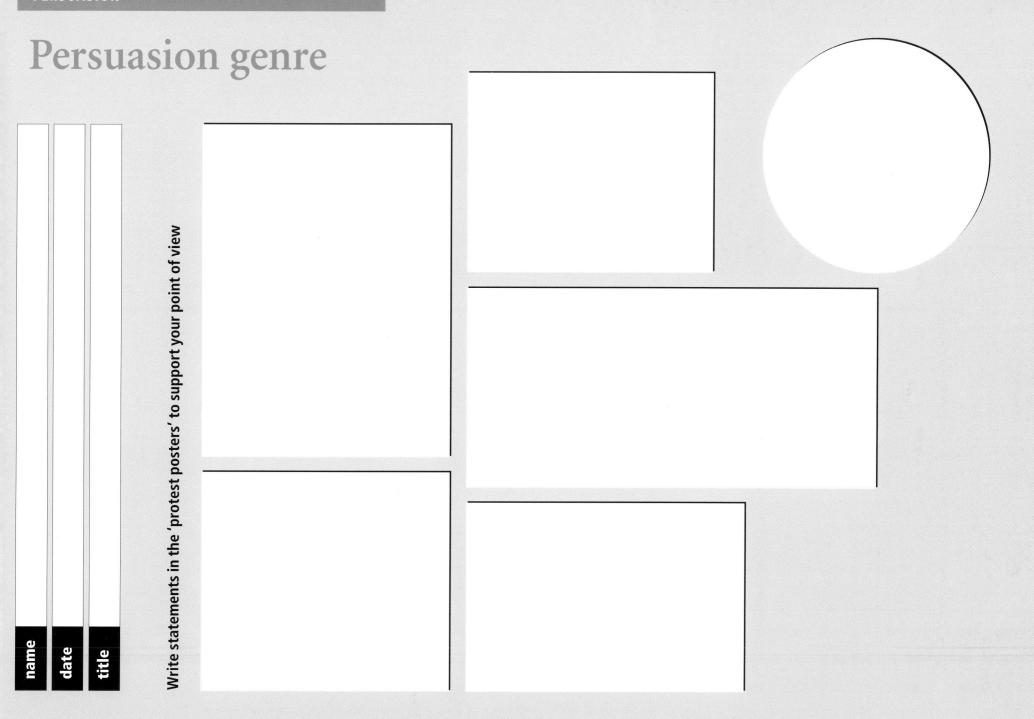

Persuasion genre

name

date

title

Although not everybody would agree, I want to argue that

I have several reasons for arguing for this point of view. My first reason is

A further reason is

Furthermore

Therefore, although some people might argue that

I think I have shown that

Persuasion genre

name

date

title

I think that

because

The reasons for my thinking this are, firstly

so

Another reason is

Moreover

because

These facts/arguments/ideas show that

Persuasion genre

name

date

title

I would like to persuade you that

There are several points I want to make to support my point of view.
Firstly

These words and phrases might help you:

because

therefore

you can see

a supporting argument

this shows that

another piece of evidence is

Discussion genre

name

date

title

The issue we are discussing is whether

Make notes in the boxes below listing the arguments for and against.
■ Remember notes are just brief outlines. They don't have to be in sentences.

Arguments against

Arguments for

My conclusion, based on the evidence, is

Now use these notes to help you write a discussion paper on this issue

Discussion genre

name

date

title

Some people think that

because

They argue that

Another group who agree with this point of view are ....

They say that

On the other hand .... disagree with the idea that
....

They claim that

They also say

My opinion is

because

Discussion genre

name

date

title

There is a lot of discussion about whether

The people who agree with this idea, such as .... claim that

They also argue that

A further point they make is

However there are also strong arguments against this point of view. .... believe that

They say that

Furthermore they claim that

After looking at the different points of view and the evidence for them I think

because